QUOTABLE
BYRON

QUOTABLE
BYRON

Words of Wisdom, Faith, and Success by
and about BYRON NELSON,
Golf's Great Ambassador

Jon Bradley

TowleHouse Publishing
Nashville, Tennessee

TowleHouse books are distributed by National Book Network
(NBN), 4720 Boston Way, Lanham, Maryland 20706.

Library of Congress Cataloging-in-Publication data is available.
ISBN: 1-931249-10-5

Cover design by Gore Studio, Inc.
Page design by Mike Towle

Printed in the United States of America
  2 3 4 5 6 — 06 05 04 03

Contents

Foreword   ix

Acknowledgments   xi

Preface   xiii

1. The Game   1

2. The Streak   21

3. Love of Golf   34

4. Faith   39

5. Caddies   44

6. Golf in the Early Years   46

7. The Tour   54

8. His Career in Golf   58

9. Early Retirement   63

10. Straight Down the Middle   71

11. The Mental Game   76

12. Competition   79

13. Teaching the Game   88

14. Ben Hogan   93

15. The Byron Nelson Classic   98

16. Life After Eighty   103

17. Friends 113

Notes 119

*To Byron Nelson, for his wonderful
influence on the lives of all
those who have known him.*

Happy 90th Birthday, Byron!

*All author's royalties from
this book are dedicated to the
Byron and Louise Nelson Golf
Endowment Fund at Abilene
Christian University,
Abilene, Texas.*

Foreword

Ever since my first year on the PGA Tour in 1981, it has been an honor to know Byron Nelson. From being the nervous rookie in 1981 to winning the GTE Byron Nelson Classic in 1999, I have continually been graced by Byron's friendly and easygoing manner, which has been an inspiration to me as well as many others.

When I was asked to write the foreword for this book, I jumped at the chance to be associated with such a great player and ambassador of the game. Everyone knows about Byron's great career, from the fifty-four victories, which included five major titles and the eleven consecutive victories in 1945, to his present-day role overseeing one of the best tournaments on the PGA Tour.

With those records, his place in golf history is secure. With this book, you get an insight to the character and integrity that brought Byron success and made him the great role model that he is.

One of the pleasures of being a past champion of his tournament in Dallas is being able to attend the past champions' dinner every year and having Byron share his stories of golf and life.

In the pages that follow you will be able to share in some of these pearls of wisdom and insight as well as other thoughts on the life of Byron Nelson. *Quotable Byron* is a great lesson on what it means to be the gentleman, Byron Nelson.

—*Loren Roberts*
1999 Byron Nelson Classic champion

Acknowledgments

There are several people who deserve special recognition for helping me with this book.

First, attempting to write any book about Byron Nelson is impossible without the help of Peggy Nelson who emptied Byron's and her house of golf books, magazines and clippings for my research. Without Peggy's help this book would have been a ninety-fifth birthday present to Byron. My good friend Tim DeBaufre, the retired pro at Philadelphia Country Club, volunteered to research the Temple University Archives and produced some great newspaper articles from the 1930's. I would also like to thank the Salesmanship Club of Dallas and especially Bette Rathjen and fellow club member and photographer Dr. John Gill for their contributions. Finding out of print golf books was easy thanks to the help of Pete Yagi who expanded my golf book collection to new levels. For typing my notes, my longtime assistant Connie Thompson again made my work look much better.

Finally and most of all thanks to my wife Debbie and son Jeff who supported me and allowed me to have my research materials all over our home all during the summer.

Preface

When people find out that I have worked with Byron Nelson for more than twenty years, they usually say, "Byron seems to be such a wonderful person. Is he as nice as he seems?" My answer is, "No, he isn't. He is really quite *nicer* than even his impeccable reputation."

Byron Nelson is a unique man. His golf records easily establish him as one of the greatest golfers of all time: the legendary eleven straight victories, fifty-four PGA wins (including five majors), and his selection as Associated Press Athlete of the Year in both 1944 and 1945. He was a fierce competitor on the golf course, but once the round was over he almost instantly resumed being the person who could just as well be your favorite uncle or your grandfather. He has never ceased to amaze people with his kindness and generosity. With his devout Christian faith, Byron exhibits a sense of humility that is rarely seen in the world of sports. Byron has often said, "I don't understand what the big deal is about me. I played some good golf, but that was an awfully long time ago."

The life lessons I have learned from Byron are too numerous to list, but one of the most important ones came in 1996. A gentleman approached Byron and myself about a Nelson endorsement of a new golf product. After making his presentation, the businessman asked Byron if he could have his endorsement and what the fee would be. Byron thought for a moment and said, "Well, if your product works, it will be good for the game of golf. I'll give you a year's endorsement for free." The gentleman was Bill Ward, the product was SoftSpikes, and it was definitely good for the game.

This book was written so the reader may come to know a very special person a little better. If you know Byron better, it will be good for the game of golf and the game of life.

—*Jon Bradley*

THE GAME

I never saw a good player from the trees.[1]

❦

The only thing that you should force in a golf swing is the club back into the bag.[2]

❦

I call my sand wedge my half-Nelson, because I can always strangle the opposition with it.[3]

❦

There are plateaus in this game, and when you reach a high one you must try to hold yourself there and expect soon to fall backward to a lower level.[4]

❦

I always had a deliberate set, and the boys like Toney Penna, Demaret, and others that knew me real well would say they knew when I was playing well because I would set the club before I made the move down.[5]

WHEN I WAS STILL AN AMATEUR, BYRON AND I PLAYED A SERIES OF EXHIBITIONS AROUND CALIFORNIA. I LEARNED A LOT DURING THAT TIME. AFTER WE PLAYED, HE WOULD GO OVER MY ROUND, ASKING ME WHY I PLAYED A CERTAIN SHOT OR HIT A CERTAIN CLUB. HE WAS TRYING TO REFINE MY PLAYING.[6]

—Ken Venturi

There's never been enough said about rhythm in the golf swing. You see, when everything is moving together, that's a pretty smooth rhythm.[7]

The only way you can improve your game is by taking the bad parts of your game and changing them.[8]

I tell a lot of people that when it comes to dealing with pressure, learn to breathe slowly and deeply. Don't let your breathing get any faster. Force yourself to walk more slowly and to take deeper, slower breaths.[9]

⌒

The mechanics of my swing were such that no thought was required. It's like eating. You don't think to feed yourself. All my concentration was on the scoring, not the swing, so I'll never know what caused it. The main thing I worried about was my tempo. Some call it timing, but I call it tempo and it's everything. I was afraid of losing it, but I couldn't lose it.[10]

⌒

I think that all of us, good and poor players alike, don't like to practice from fifty yards in. It's not exciting. Home runs are exciting, but 70 percent of your shots are played from within a hundred yards of the green.[11]

⌒

Byron shows President George Bush and Vice President Dan Quayle some pitching pointers on the White House lawn. (Photo from personal collection of Byron Nelson)

All I was trying to do was find a better way to swing so I could make a living at the game. I found a better way and, as a result, I've been credited by most experts with developing the modern way to play golf. But I sure wasn't thinking about that at the time.[12]

My foot and leg action was even looser than what they use now. I don't think many people could play as loose-kneed as I did. But it worked for me; besides, all that criticism didn't worry me as long as I was cashing those checks regularly.[13]

The fine player will never hit the ball as hard as he has to—until he has to.[14]

The best way to swing is the simplest way. Most players try to make the golf swing more difficult than it really is.[15]

~

The key thought here—and it's one of the most important you'll ever be given—is don't get too anxious to hit. Don't try to get the downswing started before the backswing is completed.[16]

~

You can't place too much emphasis on smoothness in your swing, but you can overdo the slowness.[17]

~

You'll catch yourself breathing particularly fast during moments of pressure on the course, and you'll have trouble making a good swing if that's happening. Calm down your breathing and you'll calm down your body. That will change your whole way of swinging the club.[18]

~

I wish now that I had worked at my putting game more than I did in the early days. The boys today really practice it and this helps tremendously in lowering their scores.[19]

Meeting the challenge of trouble shots is the test of a golfer. I can't think of a great one who couldn't play out of trouble or overcome unusual situations. Jack Nicklaus, for example, is the best trouble player I've ever seen.[20]

Realizing just one fact will help you become a better wind player—if you hit the ball solidly, it's amazing how little the wind will affect it.[21]

I think everyone should pattern himself after a good player. If you began playing the game as a youngster, you probably did that subconsciously—and it's still a good idea even if you have waited until adulthood to start playing. But, for heaven's sake, emulate somebody with your own size and physical characteristics.[22]

So, seniors . . . Be realistic about your capabilities now and you'll retain your ability to play well for just about as long as you want.[23]

Be aware that when the going gets rough, and you're getting a little nervous about winning the Nassau bet or the match in your club tournament, the last thing you want is to speed up your tempo and destroy your rhythm. Actually, you want to tone down your swing instead of toning it up.[24]

Bob Jones hit the nail on the head when he said that when he was thinking about three things during his swing he was playing poorly; when he was thinking about two things he had a chance to shoot par; and when he was thinking of only one thing he figured he could win the tournament.[25]

⌒

I'd tell my wife I was going to win the tournament. When she asked me how I knew, I'd tell her it was because I was hitting the ball exactly the same length every time.[26]

⌒

When I was playing, we had to learn to move the ball around and play different shots because you never knew what condition the greens would be in. A green could have hard places over here and soft spots there, and you had to play around them.[27]

⌒

I NEVER SAW BYRON HIT A SHOT ON WHICH HE LOST HIS BALANCE. REGARDLESS OF THE TERRAIN, I NEVER ONCE SAW HIM OFF BALANCE.[28]

—*Horton Smith*

A golfer, good or bad, must face reality and shortcomings like a pro and practice with honesty and patience, not to eliminate faults but to find out what his body can do and build his game around those shots.[29]

I early proved to my own satisfaction that it is next to impossible to stand too close to the ball.[30]

I had previously proven to myself that the best way to ensure a well-timed swing was to start the clubhead, hands, and shoulders back in a single motion. It seemed that when I did this, my timing turned out to be okay throughout my swing.[31]

When I finally got around to keeping that appendage
(left arm) really straight, I found that I became more
firm at the top of my backswing, and consequently
more consistent in my shot-making.[32]

It's the easiest thing in the world to blame your
golfing mistakes on factors other than yourself, but
the usual truth of the matter lies right under the
skin of the alibi expert.[33]

If there's one thing I love, it's playing golf in the rain.
Sound silly? It isn't. You see, I'm an unorthodox golfer.
It's that short swing that makes me okay in the rain. A
free swinger has to tighten up when his clothes get
wet. Whether he wants to or not. I'm already tight-
ened up. Dampness, therefore, cuts no ice.[34]

When I was a kid I was no different from anybody else. I tried to copy all of the big shots. Trouble was, I never could seem to get the hang of the way they swung their clubs. So I had to swing the way things suited me best. That's why I think I'm a self-made golfer.[35]

~

AT IMPACT BYRON'S LEFT LEG WAS NEVER STRAIGHT. MOST POWER HITTERS HAD STRAIGHT LEFT LEGS AT IMPACT, WITH EITHER THE LEFT HEEL OFF THE GROUND OR THE LEFT ANKLE BENT WAY OVER TOWARD THE TARGET. BYRON SORT OF SIDE-SLIPPED, OR SHIFTED, INTO THE HITTING AREA WITH HIS HIPS AND KNEES LEADING THE WAY.[36]

—*Jug McSpaden*

~

You'll hear a lot of people say that it's best to break in on a really tough course. I look at it just the opposite way. A difficult course, for a beginner, will make him scared of the game. There'll be so much potential trouble in sight every time he hits a ball that he's constantly tightened up, but on a course with big, broad fairways, he learns to gauge his shots properly for distance and wind conditions, to hit the ball freely. Eventually that gets bred into his game and is a fundamental part of it by the time he moves up to a real championship course.[37]

Golf is a percentage game, and I play the percentages.[38]

Ninety-nine times out of a hundred, a player's first impression of what club he needs on a certain shot or how the putt will break will be the right one. If he stands there and keeps thinking about it and changing his mind, he becomes confused, and then will usually mess up the shot.[39]

There have been more great fast players than great slow ones. Bobby Jones, Gene Sarazen, Lloyd Mangrum, Jimmy Demaret, Sam Snead—they have all been fast players.[40]

~

We were more concerned with style and with management of our shots. Today, the boys only think of one thing—scoring. They're going for birdies on every hole. Few of them are real stylists. They're home run hitters on the golf course.[41]

~

Still, I knew that I was going to miss shots. All golfers do. I couldn't eliminate that because I'm human. But the thing I could eliminate was throwing away shots.[42]

~

The harder you work, the luckier you get. (Photo from personal collection of Byron Nelson)

Bing Crosby called me that winter (1950), though, and invited me to come play in his tournament. I remember practicing my short game to get the rhythm going, and I always thought that was the most important part of golf, anyway. I wound up winning the tournament.[43]

They say when you're playing well, you get a lot of breaks—or another way of putting it, the harder you work, the luckier you get.[44]

The important thing about practice is this: Once you have mastered the mechanics of the golf swing, then you need to practice until the mechanics become second nature with you, and you need to continue practicing so that you will stay in this "groove."[45]

When you're in competition, scoring is a game of its own, and if you have to concentrate on your swing, the pressure is magnified a thousand times.[46]

⌒

The real champion will handle each circumstance as it arises, and he can win on any course.[47]

⌒

I have often said that there is no such person as a good iron player out of the rough.[48]

⌒

One of the worst faults of the average golfer is to bring the hands into play too soon, causing a distinct loss of clubhead speed.[49]

⌒

Hitting those high shots that land softly really paid off for me over the years at Augusta.[50]

~

The long iron is a much-misunderstood club. If you will just swing it with the same ease with which you swing your woods, your troubles will be over.[51]

~

Once you find something in your swing that works and is fundamentally sound, stay with it. If your game goes sour, resist the temptation to fool with that fundamental. For the average golfer, experimenting is death.[52]

~

But after developing a shortness of swing—I did so to eliminate some looseness and make my swing more compact, and I think that's the best way a tall person can do it—I learned I had to get a full turn of my shoulders to get any distance.[53]

~

I'd say the first thing to do when you begin serious work on your game, after you have the swing you want, is learn how to hit the ball square and hit it straight.[54]

⌒

The only danger in experimenting is not knowing when to stop.[55]

⌒

I was twenty-four years old when I more or less quit experimenting.[56]

⌒

The reason we practice is to get our swing so automatic that we don't have to think about the mechanics of a swing when we're trying to score.[57]

⌒

A word about putting in general. Too many players think too much about the mechanical part of the putting stroke, rather than getting the feel and thinking about the speed. Putting is mostly feel and confidence.[58]

Among the many reasons most people fail to play golf as well as they would like is the fact that they are so wrapped up in the technique of hitting the ball that they tend to ignore the technique of playing the game.[59]

20

THE STREAK

THE MOST UNFAIR COMMENT IS THAT NELSON HAD NO COM-
PETITION IN 1945. SNEAD WAS AROUND THE WHOLE YEAR.
HOGAN MADE SEVENTEEN STARTS AND FINISHED FIRST, SEC-
OND, OR THIRD IN TWELVE OF THEM.[1]

—Bill Inglish, former Masters statistician

⌒

MOST OVERLOOKED IS HIS THREE-YEAR RECORD FOR 1944, '45,
AND '46. IN SEVENTY-FIVE STARTS HE WON THIRTY-FOUR
TIMES, OR 45 PERCENT. HE FINISHED FIRST OR SECOND FIFTY
TIMES, OR TWO-THIRDS OF THE TIME.[2]

—Bill Inglish

⌒

I TAKE THE VIEW THAT "THE STREAK" REALLY LASTED TWO AND A HALF YEARS. I CLAIM IT STRETCHES FROM JANUARY OF 1944 THROUGH JULY OF 1946, THE MONTH WHEN BYRON OFFICIALLY RETIRED. IT WAS DURING THIS PERIOD THAT NELSON WAS THE MOST DOMINANT PLAYER THE PROFESSIONAL GAME HAS EVER KNOWN.[3]

—*Dan Jenkins*

I was a good lag putter, I rarely three-putted, and I made a lot of fifteen- and twenty-footers, but for some reason I wasn't very good from six to ten feet.[4]

I was confident I could always hit the fairway with my driver, and I felt I could just do anything with the five-iron. Hit it anywhere from 130 to 180 yards, and put it right where I wanted it. I guess it's because the five-iron was the first club I ever owned as a kid (that) I played a lot of rounds of golf with a five-iron only.[5]

The important thing to me during that time was that I scored well and played very consistently. That year (1945) I played 127 rounds, and 73 was my highest score. I had nineteen consecutive rounds under 70, and I averaged 68.3.[6]

DURING HIS STREAK YEAR OF 1945, BYRON WAS MAGICAL. HE COULDN'T SEEM TO PLAY A BAD ROUND. THE PRESSURE WAS AMAZING, BUT BYRON HANDLED IT WITH HIS USUAL GRACE. HIS APPROACH WAS INTERESTING. HE HAD GROOVED HIS SWING AND WAS PRETTY HAPPY WITH IT, SO DURING THE STREAK HE STOPPED PRACTICING.[7]

—*Sam Snead*

Except for the prize money, the only contract I got the year of the Streak was with Wheaties for two hundred dollars and a case of Wheaties a month (for six months).[8]

GOLF FANS WERE CERTAINLY SURPRISED AT WHAT HE DID THAT YEAR, BUT [JIMMY] DEMARET, SNEAD—ALL THE GUYS HE PLAYED AGAINST—WERE STUNNED.[9]

—*Dave Marr*

THE COURSES IN THE FORTIES WEREN'T AS LONG, BUT THE GREENS WEREN'T AS GOOD, EITHER. THE GREENS WEREN'T AS GOOD AS THE FAIRWAYS ARE NOW. AND I DON'T CARE IF SOME OF THE PLAYERS WERE IN THE SERVICE OR OVERSEAS— THE SECRET TO THE WHOLE THING WAS HIS SCORING AVER- AGE. WHAT WAS IT, 68.3? YOU COULDN'T DO THAT IF THEY GAVE YOU ALL YOUR TEN-FOOT PUTTS.[10]

—*Don January*

WHAT IS IT LIKE TO WIN A LOT OF TOURNAMENTS IN A ROW? EXHAUSTING. BEING IN CONTENTION EVERY WEEK IS EXHAUSTING, TO BEGIN WITH. THEN WHEN YOU START WINNING, THE PRESSURE BUILDS SO MUCH, YOU WANT TO CRAWL INTO A HOLE. SO WHAT BYRON DID WAS MIND-BOGGLING. AWE INSPIRING.[11]

—*Mickey Wright*

I beat (Ben) Hogan in Miami and then the next week beat Snead. I knew I was playing well, and I was feeling pretty good.[12]

I was playing very well, and with each win I was getting more and more confidence. I (was) also getting a lot of requests for exhibitions. So I'm finishing one tournament and then going someplace to play an exhibition for three hundred dollars. For that three hundred dollars I had to put on a clinic, stay for lunch, play eighteen holes, and a lot of times stay and make a talk at a dinner. But that was big money for me then.[13]

REGARDLESS OF COMPETITION, ELEVEN CONSECUTIVE WINS IS ALMOST A MIRACLE IF YOU'RE COMPETING AGAINST CAR WASH ATTENDANTS PLAYING CROSSHANDED IN TENNIS SHOES. PART OF THE TIME, ALL THINGS CONSIDERED, YOU'RE GOING TO BEAT YOURSELF.[14]

—*Blackie Sherrod, writer*

SOMEBODY COULD HAVE GOTTEN HOT JUST LIKE I DID
(69-69-64-68), BUT IF YOU LOOK AT BYRON'S SCORING RECORD,
IT WAS PHENOMENAL. I JUST DON'T THINK YOU CAN TAKE
AWAY FROM HIS GREAT STREAK. I SAW HIM SHOOT SEVERAL
ROUNDS OF 65 WHERE HE HIT ALL THE PAR-FIVES IN TWO. I
NEVER SAW HIM PLAY A ROUND WHERE HE DIDN'T KNOCK
ONE TO TWO BALLS WITHIN A FOOT OF THE CUP.[15]

—*Fred Haas Jr.*

IN 1945 BYRON NELSON WAS THE GREATEST GOLFER OF ALL
TIME. THE MAN WON ELEVEN TOURNAMENTS IN A ROW.
SOME PEOPLE SAY IT WAS THE WAR AND LACK OF COMPETI-
TION, BUT THAT'S BULL. IN 1945 BYRON NELSON WAS AS
CLOSE TO A MACHINE AS ANYONE WHO EVER PLAYED GOLF.[16]

—*Arnold Palmer*

I became confident. I realized I could do with the golf ball pretty much what I wanted to do . . . Everybody wanted to talk to me—that was the toughest part.[17]

I was playing with blinders. I drove very well, reached the greens easily, and just kept rolling.[18]

Mangrum, Hogan, Snead, Sarazen, Demaret. There were a lot of good players in my era. We were not exactly hackers.[19]

The Streak means a tremendous amount to me. When I was playing and winning those tournaments, I didn't think about being in a streak. I trained myself to play one stroke, one hole, one tournament at a time.[20]

YET HISTORY HAS TREATED NELSON SOMEWHAT GRUDGINGLY.
THE RECORD OF HIS DEEDS REMAINS HEROIC, BUT HIS STORY
HAS NEVER TAKEN ON THE PROPORTIONS OF A PROPER
LEGEND. THE TROUBLE IS THAT NELSON MADE IT ALL
SEEM SO SINFULLY EASY.[21]

—*Sarah Pileggi, writer*

I DON'T GIVE A DAMN HOW MANY PEOPLE PLAYED. I DON'T
CARE IF THERE HAD BEEN THIRTY MORE PLAYERS EVERY WEEK
OR WHAT THEIR NAMES WERE. THERE STILL WOULD NOT
HAVE BEEN ANYONE ELSE WINNING.[22]

—*Jug McSpaden*

NO WAY ANYONE EVER WILL COME CLOSE TO BYRON'S
RECORD.[23]

—*Ben Crenshaw*

The best thing about the Streak is that now people talk to me all the time about it. A long time ago, it wasn't mentioned as much. And nobody ever talks to me now about losing tournaments. They talk about winning. They don't ask what happened in not winning the PGA or Masters anymore. That's a big plus for me.[24]

Smooth and silky, just like always. (Photo from personal collection of Byron Nelson)

I DON'T CARE IF HE WAS PLAYING AGAINST ORANGUTANS, WINNING ELEVEN STRAIGHT IS AMAZING.[25]

—*Jackie Burke Jr.*

I look back on it now, and it just seems like a good long dream. I don't know, I must have played over my head for a period of a year and a half or so. But you know, the thing was, I consistently drove the ball in the fairway, and when you're doing that, you've got to be swinging well enough to put the ball on the green with your irons.[26]

I REMEMBER MY DAD TELLING ME (NELSON) WON ELEVEN STRAIGHT. THAT'S WHAT YOU CALL A HOT STREAK.[27]

—*Tiger Woods*

IF BYRON HADN'T BEEN BORN, I MIGHT HAVE BEEN A GREAT
PLAYER.[28]

*—Jug McSpaden, who finished
runner-up to Nelson seven times in 1945*

One other thing I should mention. My game had got-
ten so good and so dependable that there were times
when I actually would get bored playing. I'd hit it in
the fairway, on the green, make birdie or par, and go to
the next hole. The press even said it was monotonous
to watch me. I'd tell them, "It may be monotonous,
but I sure eat regular."[29]

BUT IN GOLF THERE IS ALWAYS OLD MAN PAR TO TEST THE
CALIBER OF THE PLAYERS, AND IN 1944 NELSON AND
MCSPADEN DID THINGS TO PAR NO GOLFERS HAD EVER DONE
IN THE AGE OF JONES OR WHEN THE POST-DEPRESSION PACK
ROARED FIFTY-STRONG AROUND THE CIRCUIT.[30]

—Herbert Warren Wind, writer

A TOP-TWENTY PLAYER HAS A 4.31 PERCENT CHANCE OF
WINNING ANY GIVEN TOURNAMENT. TO FIGURE THE
PROBABILITY OF WINNING ELEVEN CONSECUTIVE TOURNA-
MENTS, MULTIPLY THE PROBABILITY OF WINNING ONE
TOURNAMENT BY ITSELF ELEVEN TIMES. THE RESULT: THE
ODDS OF A TOP-TWENTY PLAYER WINNING ELEVEN
CONSECUTIVE TOURNAMENTS ARE 1,052,000,000,000,000-TO-1.[31]

—*Dallas Morning News*

One of these days, I'll wake up and realize it was a
dream in my own mind. I can't believe it. It amazes
me. But I've got the papers and books to prove it
happened.[32]

LOVE OF GOLF

I was incurably infected with golf.[1]

⌒

Even when I caddied for people, I loved anything that had to do with swinging a club.[2]

⌒

Perhaps more than any other sport, golf remains a game of etiquette and sportsmanship.[3]

⌒

Golf is like life in many ways. For example, when you make a decision, you should stick with it.[4]

⌒

NELSON MAY THINK HE'S BEEN BLESSED, BUT THE FACT IS THAT HE EARNED EVERYTHING THAT HE GOT OUT OF GOLF BY GIVING EVERYTHING HE COULD TO IT. YOU'D THINK, BY NOW, THE DEBTS WOULD BE REPAID. MAYBE SO, BUT NELSON IS STILL GIVING. THANKS, BYRON, GOLF COULD DO WITH MORE LIKE YOU.[5]

—*Pat Seelig, writer*

BYRON HAS DONE SO MUCH FOR GOLF. EVERYBODY KNOWS WHAT A GREAT CAREER HE HAD AS A PLAYER. BUT HE HAS CONTRIBUTED SO MUCH OFF THE COURSE. HE HAS TOTAL DEVOTION TO THE GAME. HE WILL GO ANYWHERE AND DO ANYTHING IF THERE IS A WORTHY CAUSE, AND I'M NOT TALKING ABOUT GOING FOR A BIG FEE. HE JUST LOVES THE GAME.[6]

—*Felix McKnight, retired newspaper executive*

Golf is played in a healthy environment. I don't know many kids who play a lot of golf and who also get in much trouble.[7]

BYRON NELSON IS THE EPITOME OF THE GAME. HE'S A GOOD FRIEND OF MINE. HE TREATS PEOPLE WITH RESPECT. AND HE'S ONE OF THE GREATEST PLAYERS EVER TO PLAY.[8]

—*Tom Watson*

I'LL ALWAYS ADMIRE BYRON NELSON BECAUSE HE WAS A GREAT PLAYER AND A MAN WHO HAS TAKEN TIME TO GIVE SOMETHING BACK TO THE GAME.[9]

—*Gary Player*

HE'S ONE OF THOSE PEOPLE YOU FEEL YOU'VE BEEN PRIVILEGED TO KNOW. HE'S ONE OF THE REASONS GOLF REMAINS SUCH A STRONG CHARACTER GAME. THE WAY HE'S LIVED HIS LIFE IS BIGGER THAN HIS GOLF ACCOMPLISHMENTS.[10]

—*Ben Crenshaw*

The game of golf is great in itself. You can play it no matter what your age or skill level.[11]

⌒〜

That's a funny thing about golf—even when we play well, we know there are shots we missed.[12]

⌒〜

I owe a lot of my financial success in life to golf. Not just because of the money I won—in fact, that was the least part of it—but because of all the wonderful people I met who have helped me in so many ways. Really, it's one of the best things about the game, that you can meet so many excellent people. As I said earlier, I've been a blessed man all my life, and one of the greatest blessings I have are my friends. And it just has always kept getting better and better.[13]

⌒〜

One of several reasons golf as a sport is so steadily expanding beyond others is its adaptability to all sizes, shapes, circumstances, and ages.

What makes golf the greatest of all games, is this: You can play it when you are ten, and you can play it when you are eighty. You can play with good players or you can play with poor ones. There is no other game in the world like that.[14]

It was an accident that I found the game. I was fortunate.[15]

FAITH

When you believe in Christ and believe the Word, you just have to do some of these things, that's all. That's what life's all about—what you stand for.[1]

⟨ornament⟩

BYRON AND LOUISE NELSON ARE EXAMPLES OF WHAT PEOPLE CAN BECOME WHEN THEY LIVE A LIFE OF SERVICE TO OTHERS.[2]

—Tom Landry

⟨ornament⟩

I think the only reason I have a good reputation is I've tried to do what the Bible says. I've been considered a role model for a very long time. I wouldn't do anything, and there's not enough money in the world, to cause me to break that down now.[3]

⟨ornament⟩

Winning at golf and collecting trophies became the norm for Byron at an early age. (Photo from personal collection of Byron Nelson)

BYRON HAS BEEN AS CONSISTENT IN LIFE AS HE WAS IN GOLF. HE HAS A GREAT SENSE OF BALANCE ABOUT LIFE. HE INVESTED HIMSELF IN THE RIGHT THINGS. HE SHOWS US THAT YOU ARE NEVER TOO YOUNG, OR TOO OLD, TO DEMONSTRATE YOUR FAITH BY REACHING OUT TO PEOPLE WITH RESPECT.[4]

—*Jim Sheard and Wally Armstrong, authors*

I prefer being remembered as being friendly and a good Christian man than as being a good golfer. I don't think I know anybody who has as many friends as I do. It's very gratifying.[5]

I didn't live a perfect life; I made some mistakes that I wish I hadn't made. But when I made a mistake, I tried to rectify it and not make the same one again.

It's like on the golf course, you're going to make some mistakes. I don't care how good you are, you're going to hit some bad shots. And you're going to make some mistakes in life.[6]

~

Regardless of where you are or what you are doing, someone is watching you. And I think people with notoriety have more of a responsibility to do right and be a role model because more people are watching them.[7]

~

None of us realizes how many people we influence.[8]

~

I feel I can never be as good as people think I am. But I try hard to be a Christian and do right, and all I can really do is say, "Thank you."[9]

~

After all, life is short, but eternity is forever. And I hope to not spend eternity in the wrong place.[10]

CADDIES

In those days, there were twice as many caddies as players, and the older boys made it pretty tough on any fresh kid trying to break into the bag-carrying business.

I was put through kangaroo court two or three times, made to run the gauntlet, and rolled down the hill in a barrel. But I wanted in on the easy money, so I kept going back each week.[1]

The very first time I started here (Glen Garden Country Club, in Fort Worth), I had gone through the training and Mr. Shute asked me if I could spot golf balls. Well, the very first hole, he hits a ball, and I lost it. Wouldn't you have known it?[2]

HE GOT THE GOOD BAGS WHEN HE WAS A KID CADDYING AT FORT WORTH'S GLEN GARDEN COUNTRY CLUB BECAUSE HE WAS SAYING "YES, SIR" AND "NO, SIR" WHEN ASKED QUESTIONS BY THE MEMBERS.[3]

—*Pat Seelig, writer*

BYRON'S CADDIE TROD ON HIS BALL AND THE PENALTY STROKE MIGHT HAVE MADE ALL THE DIFFERENCE. THE CADDIE WEPT; BYRON NELSON PUT HIS ARM AROUND HIS SHOULDERS AND SAID: "IT'S ALL RIGHT, SON. I WAS A CADDIE ONCE MYSELF. IT COULD HAVE HAPPENED TO ME."[4]

—*Peter Alliss, referring to the 1946 U.S. Open*

I'm saddened by the fact that the caddie is a dying breed.[5]

GOLF IN THE EARLY YEARS

I guess the best thing that ever happened to me was hard times.[1]

⌒

Aggravating that perpetual financial pinch through my first three years as a play-for-pay boy was my penchant for blaming my lack of success not on myself (as I should have done) but on my clubs. Unfortunately, they couldn't speak up to let me know what a fool I was making of myself.[2]

⌒

BYRON, WE'VE BEEN MARRIED OVER A YEAR. I HAVEN'T BOUGHT A NEW DRESS OR A NEW PAIR OF SHOES OR ANYTHING FOR MYSELF IN ALL THAT TIME. BUT YOU'VE BOUGHT FOUR NEW DRIVERS, AND YOU'RE NOT HAPPY WITH ANY OF THEM. ONE OF TWO THINGS—EITHER YOU DON'T KNOW WHAT KIND OF DRIVER YOU WANT, OR YOU DON'T KNOW HOW TO DRIVE.[3]

—*Louise Nelson, Byron's first wife,*
who passed away in 1985

⌒

Back in the days before fancy buffets greeted tour players at the clubhouse, a golfer often had to make do with a Coke and hot dog. (Photo from personal collection of Byron Nelson)

I kind of expected that Bobby (Cruickshank) would thank me or compliment my game some way. After all, he'd won fifty or sixty dollars, and I had another silver cup. But all he said was, "Laddie, if ye don't larn to grip the club right, ye'll niver make a good player."[4]

I played a lot of golf with a man at the club named Arthur Temple. Par at the Texarkana Country Club was 73, and when I played with Mr. Temple he would bet me a dollar I couldn't break par. If I broke par I got a dollar; if I didn't, why, he got a dollar. So any time I won, I could have a date with Louise.[5]

Our players all had these beautiful matching outfits—shirts, jackets, slacks, shoes, golf bags. At that time I had practically just the clothes on my back to wear. I made up my mind right then that I was going to be on the Ryder Cup team someday. Besides wanting to play for my country, I wanted the clothes and the stuff that went with it.[6]

It was said at one time you could pick the Walker Cup team out of Texas, and the reason for it was we didn't have watered fairways and we had hard greens, and you had to learn to play on all of them.[7]

I'm lucky, I've said it before, and I say it now that I've won it myself, a man has got to be lucky to win this championship (U.S. Open).[8]

~

So with different grasses on the greens and inconsistent watering, when it came to the short game, most of the pros worked on pitching and chipping and very little on putting. It just didn't pay to spend a lot of time on putting. We concentrated more on getting our approach shots as close to the pin as possible.[9]

~

Whenever I was going to a tournament, especially a match-play tournament, I would call these guys and get a game with three of them and play their best ball. We'd just play for a dollar, but it was tough. I'd shoot in the mid-60s to break even.[10]

~

WE'D GO TO PLAY AN EXHIBITION BETWEEN TOURNAMENTS, AND WE'D HAVE LUNCH WITH THE GOLF COMMITTEE. "WHAT WILL YOU SHOOT, BYRON?" THEY'D ASK. BYRON WOULD SAY, "MAY I SEE A SCORECARD?" AND "ARE THESE YARDAGES HONEST?" THEN HE'D SAY, "I BELIEVE I'LL SHOOT A 63, OR A 65." AND THEN HE'D DO IT.[11]

—*Jug McSpaden*

People ask me if I wish I were playing now, with all the money on the tour, and I can definitely say I loved playing golf when I did.

Golf was fun, then. Everybody was buddy-buddy. And when times were bad, everybody was trying to help each other make a living.[12]

They didn't have the green jacket ceremony (at the Masters) in those days. I don't know when it started. Bobby Jones handled the presentation, and I was standing there feeling nine feet tall just to think that Bobby Jones was making an award to me.[13]

⌒

ONE OF THE FINEST COMPLIMENTS ANY TWO GOLFERS EVER WERE PAID CAME WHEN BYRON NELSON AND BEN HOGAN PLAYED OFF FOR THE MASTERS IN 1942. JUST ABOUT THE WHOLE TOURNAMENT FIELD STAYED OVER TO WATCH THEM, AND ONE OF THE REASONS WAS WE COULD WALK ALONG AND KIBITZ SHOTS AND TALK TO EACH OTHER, AND TO BEN AND BYRON AS THEY PLAYED. I REMEMBER SEEING TOMMY ARMOUR, RALPH GULDAHL, JIMMY THOMSON, WILLIE GOGGIN, BOBBY CRUICKSHANK, JUG MCSPADEN, AND HENRY PICARD, JUST TO NAME A FEW, IN THE GALLERY THAT FOLLOWED BYRON AND BEN. WHY DID WE STAY? WELL, THEY WERE ABOUT THE TWO GREATEST PLAYERS IN THE WORLD AT THE TIME.[14]

—Jimmy Demaret

⌒

What Louise and I were happiest about was the fact that we could travel together again. McSpaden was okay as a traveling partner, but I definitely preferred Louise.[15]

THE TOUR

The tour is not a normal life.[1]

I didn't think of the tour as something glamorous. I just wanted to play to beat somebody. My parents didn't know much about golf, but they gave me their blessing. They said, "Be a good man and do right."[2]

Obviously, we weren't playing just for the money sometimes, more for the fun of it and the chance to keep working on our games. Back then, you learned to play winning golf by playing on the tour.[3]

Very few people today realize what it was like to be on the tour then. You didn't make enough money, even if you were a fine player, to make a living or ever accumulate anything just playing in tournaments, so it was necessary to have a club job.[4]

⌒

When we played, we played to win, and we played to build a name. And I am now being paid for what I did in my career.[5]

⌒

In those years, nobody talked about "major" championships, but the four biggest tournaments were the U.S. Open, the PGA, the Met Open, and the Western Open.[6]

⌒

Never in my wildest dreams did I imagine that professional golf would become this big. But it has for good reason and can continue to for the same reason, if these players continue to respect what they've got and the people who make it possible, the sponsors who put up a lot of the money. Be good to them, and they'll be good to you.[7]

We had to play every week to make a living. I bet if you took all I won for my career except 1945 and subtracted my expenses, I know I'd be in the negative.[8]

People ask me if Tiger could win the Grand Slam. If anybody could, he could. I have a lot of fun watching him play. I think the world of the young man. I just think he's great for the game.[9]

Today it is titles and money. We played because we loved to play. We were family, really. Today the players see each other only at the first tee and practice tee. In our day, when we left Phoenix, Louise and I would tell Valerie and Ben (Hogan) we'd stop at Las Cruces, New Mexico, at a little bus stop that specialized in tamales.[10]

HIS CAREER IN GOLF

Back then, to be successful in the golf business in any way, you had to get a club job in the East.[1]

⌒

HE WAS THE BEST TWO-WOOD PLAYER TO THE GREEN THAT I EVER SAW. IF THERE WERE SIXTEEN PAR-FIVE HOLES IN A TOURNAMENT, YOU COULD BET HE WOULD BE TEN TO TWELVE UNDER PAR FOR THOSE HOLES.[2]

—*Jug McSpaden*

⌒

At impact I had a tendency to dip my knees, in the style of many tall players. Early in my career Gene Sarazen told me I'd never make a great golfer because my knees were not straight enough through impact. If I had listened to Gene and changed, no telling what might have happened.[3]

⌒

Byron's knees helping keep the club on line. (Photo from personal collection of Byron Nelson)

I always had the reputation of being at my best with the long irons. But that's only based on one shot—the one-iron I holed in the play-off against Craig Wood at Spring Mill for the '39 National Open. The fact is, the driver is the one club I could most depend on.[4]

Well, I did not putt badly, but the length Nicklaus was great at, eight to ten feet, was my weakness. I lagged longer putts pretty well. I didn't three-putt much. But the best part of my game was the long game. Snead said I was the best driver that he played against. I drove the ball in play an awful lot and I drove an average of 254 yards, which was long then. I had a reputation as being a good long-iron player. But my basic game was a steady game. I wasn't bad at any of it.[5]

I'm genuinely sorry that I never made a real effort to win the British Open. When I was in competition, I didn't think too much about it, but since then I've wished a thousand times I had gone to England. In those days I refused to fly, because I didn't like it. And since I was the world's worst sailor, I didn't want to try an overseas trip.[6]

~

There's no question in my mind that the best golf I ever played, and I didn't win the tournament, was when I tied for the National Open in 1946 at Canterbury. That was the tournament when the caddie kicked the ball in the fairway and I got a penalty stroke that put me in a tie.[7]

~

By 1957 I had been off the tour for quite a number of years, but I decided to play in the Masters and was having a pretty good tournament. I was paired with Peter Thomson in the final round and came to the sixteenth hole at even par. My tee shot was right on line but it spun back off the green and into the water. I moved to the front of the tee and changed clubs, hitting a seven-iron. The ball went into the cup on the fly, bounced out, spun back through the bunker and into the water. I took another drop, got the ball on the green, and took two putts for a seven. Do you know the ovation I got when I walked off the green was as loud as any I ever got for winning a tournament?[8]

EARLY RETIREMENT

I got sick and tired of competing. I never looked back. Nobody understands it, but I never did feel I quit too soon. I accomplished everything I set out to do.[1]

⌒

I'm not getting younger, and I know too well that I could go down in my business. I have always wanted a farm where I could raise whiteface cattle. Now I have it, I am happy.[2]

⌒

I AM THE GIRL WHO VOWED NEVER TO MARRY A GOLFER OR A FARMER.[3]

—*Louise Nelson*

⌒

Home on the range in Roanoke, Texas. (Photo from personal collection of Byron Nelson)

I'm just tired. It has been a long grind. There were days when I thought I would scream if I had to go to the course. It was week in and week out for years. I tried to give my best to golf. Now I want to realize a boyhood dream. I've got 500 pasture acres and 130 more under cultivation.[4]

Build a golf course out here? Listen, anybody who even mentions golf around the farm for a while could get shot.[5]

I SAID OKAY JUST AS WE WALKED THROUGH THE LOBBY OF THE HOTEL WE WERE CHECKING INTO. BYRON DIDN'T EVEN PUT DOWN HIS GOLF CLUBS. HE WENT STRAIGHT TO THE PHONE AND CLOSED THE PURCHASE (ON FAIRWAY RANCH).[6]

—*Louise Nelson*

I fell in love with this place the first time I saw it. And once we'd given them the money and signed the papers, and the ranch belonged to us, nothing else really mattered. I knew I didn't want to leave. And so I never did.[7]

Feeding his cattle. (Photo from personal collection of Byron Nelson)

MY VIEW OF BYRON'S CAREER IS THAT IT WAS A BIT LIKE
BOBBY JONES'S. JONES WON THE GRAND SLAM. AND THEN
HE CALLED IT QUITS. THERE WERE NO OTHER WORLDS TO
CONQUER.[8]

—*Sam Snead*

The one tournament that had eluded me, which I'd
thrown away twice, was the Los Angeles Open. If I
hadn't won that in 1946, I probably would have played
another year. But my goal was to win every important
tournament in the United States.[9]

Leaving the tour like I did basically was the best thing
that ever happened to Byron Nelson. For one thing, I
might never have gotten my ranch. But also for two
other reasons: I never would have become the first golfer
to work television or the first to have his own tourna-
ment. Things like that come along but once in life.[10]

LOOKING BACK ON IT I REALIZE I WAS BEING SELFISH. BUT ANYWAY, HE GOT HIMSELF BUSY AND HE MADE A LOT OF MONEY. THAT WAS 1945. WHEN HE HAD SAVED UP OVER FIFTY THOUSAND DOLLARS IN CASH, HE THOUGHT HE COULD START LOOKING. BUT IT WASN'T ENOUGH MONEY, AND I SAID, "WELL, YOU'RE JUST GOING TO HAVE TO WORK ANOTH-ER YEAR. YOU'LL HAVE TO WORK THROUGH THE NATIONAL OPEN." WE MADE A PACT WE WOULDN'T TELL ANYONE, AND WE DIDN'T. HE ALMOST WON THAT OPEN. IT WAS WHEN HIS CADDIE STEPPED ON HIS BALL.[11]

—*Louise Nelson*

I look at it this way. I left before I ever suffered that one really crushing defeat. That means nobody ever talks to me about losing. They only talk to me about winning.[12]

I finally had to admit I'd accomplished everything I'd set out to do in golf. It was time to move on.[13]

STRAIGHT DOWN THE MIDDLE

If you don't think straight, you won't hit straight.[1]

◦~

AT ATLANTA, NELSON CAME UP TO ME AND SAID, "YOU KNOW, A FUNNY THING HAPPENED THIS LAST ROUND. I PLAYED TWO SHOTS OUT OF THE DIVOT MARKS I MADE THE ROUND BEFORE." THAT'S CONSISTENCY.[2]

—*Fred Corcoran, tournament organizer*

◦~

HE COULD PLAY A BALL UP TIMES SQUARE, AND JUST USE THE SIDEWALKS, AT THAT.[3]

—*Fred Corcoran*

◦~

OLDER AND WISER, I CAN NOW BETTER APPRECIATE BYRON'S TALENT FOR SPLINTERING THE PINS AS WELL AS HIS STYLE OF PLAYING MORE QUICKLY THAN ANYBODY I'VE EVER SEEN.[4]

—*Dan Jenkins*

◦~

THERE WAS A NEW IRRIGATION SYSTEM IN THE FAIRWAY WHERE HE WAS HITTING, AND I'LL NEVER FORGET SITTING WITH OTHER KIDS WATCHING SHOT AFTER SHOT, WITH ALL THE CLUBS, DROP SMACK ON THE LINE WHERE THE CENTER PIPING WAS LAID. IT WAS INCREDIBLE . . . AWESOME, AS THEY SAY TODAY . . . AND STILL THE FINEST EXHIBITION OF GOLFING ACCURACY I'VE EVER WITNESSED.[5]

—*Jack Nicklaus*

BYRON PROBABLY WAS THE GREATEST STRIKER OF THE BALL, THE GREATEST PLAYER THE GAME HAS EVER KNOWN. THAT'S OPEN TO DEBATE, OF COURSE—BUT MY FATHER SAID SO.[6]

—*Tom Watson*

WE WERE PAIRED TOGETHER AT COLONIAL AND I WAS A LITTLE NERVOUS . . . HE HIT THE FLAG TWICE THAT DAY WITH FULL IRON SHOTS. THE WAY HE GRIPPED THE CLUB, THE WAY HE LINED UP, YOU KNEW HE COULD START THE MOTOR RUNNING AGAIN IF HE WANTED TO. HE LOOKED LIKE A MASTER CRAFTSMAN.[7]

—*Dave Marr*

That little dip they talked about in my swing happened because my knees were staying flexed and moving laterally farther than usual. I might not recommend that much leg action for everybody, but it had its advantages for me. I once went to Purdue University, where they took some pictures of me and four other leading players of the time. Those pictures proved that my club was on line longer and lower going back and through than any of the others. I think that's another reason why my shots had less curvature to them.[8]

NELSON WAS A MIRACLE OF CONSISTENCY. AT HIS PEAK BYRON ERRED SO INFREQUENTLY THAT IT COULD BE BORING TO WATCH HIM. HE MADE GOOD GOLF LOOK AS EASY AS VARDON DID, ALTHOUGH HE LACKED THE GRACE OF HARRY, AND OF JONES, AS WELL. BYRON WAS A PROFICIENT RATHER THAN A PRETTY GOLFER. LACK OF ERROR WAS WHAT HE AIMED FOR AND ACHIEVED BY REDUCING SHOT-MAKING TO A MINIMUM OF FUNDAMENTALS.[9]

—*Herbert Warren Wind*

BYRON AT THAT TIME MAY HAVE BEEN THE MOST CONSUM-MATE TEE-SHOT ARTIST THE GAME HAS EVER KNOWN. HE DIDN'T JUST DRIVE WITH HIS DRIVER, HE PLAYED SHOTS WITH IT, INTENTIONALLY HOOKING OR SLICING THE BALL AROUND DOGLEGS, OR DRAWING AND FADING IT INTO SOME PARTICULAR NOOK OF FAIRWAY WHICH HE THOUGHT GAVE HIM THE WISEST SHOT TO THE GREEN. IN THE PROCESS, THIS MAN WOULD GO WEEKS, NOT JUST DAYS, WITHOUT MISSING A FAIRWAY, AND WHEN YOU CAME TO A PAR-FIVE HIS DRIVES SUDDENLY BECAME TWENTY TO THIRTY YARDS LONGER THAN USUAL.[10]

—*Charles Price, writer*

I FONDLY REMEMBER HARVEY PENICK'S SAYING ONE TIME THAT THE PROOF OF THIS WAS THAT BYRON'S DIVOTS LOOKED LIKE DOLLAR BILLS. FOR BYRON TO TAKE DIVOTS SO THIN, SO LONG, AND SO PERFECTLY RECTANGULAR, HE HAD TO KEEP THE BLADE ABSOLUTELY SQUARE FOR A LONG, LONG TIME THROUGH IMPACT.[11]

—*Ben Crenshaw*

NOBODY KEPT THE BALL ON THE CLUBFACE LONGER
THROUGH IMPACT THAN BYRON DID. HE TOOK THE CLUB
BACK STRAIGHT AWAY FROM THE BALL WITH THAT UPRIGHT
SWING OF HIS, THEN EXTENDED THROUGH IT IN A WAY
WHERE THE CLUBHEAD MOVED ALONG THE TARGET LINE
FOR A GOOD DISTANCE AFTER IMPACT. THIS MADE HIM
AMAZINGLY ACCURATE AND CONSISTENT.[12]

—Ken Venturi

BYRON WAS VERY INFLUENTIAL IN MY CAREER. I USED TO
CADDIE FOR HIM AND SHAG HIS PRACTICE SESSIONS WHEN
HE WAS THE PRO IN TEXARKANA. WE'D PLAY MATCHES FOR A
DIME, BUT WHAT I REMEMBER MOST IS WATCHING HIM PRAC-
TICE. I'VE NEVER SEEN ANYONE HIT THE BALL SO CONSIS-
TENTLY STRAIGHT. I THINK THE REAL REASON I WENT BALD
SO FAST IS THAT HE KEPT BOUNCING BALLS OFF MY HEAD.[13]

—Miller Barber

THE MENTAL GAME

As soon as you believe it can be done, a great psychological barrier is broken and you begin to work toward higher goals. That's what the players started to do after Arnold (Palmer) showed them the way and that's what they do today.[1]

～

Do the putts you should be holing in the two- to six-foot range, and teach yourself to make putts. Don't practice a real difficult putt, because that will destroy your confidence. Subconsciously, you'll begin to feel you can't make a putt.[2]

～

Play within yourself. But don't play defensively or hesitantly. Think that you're going to hit each shot well instead of trying not to hit it badly.[3]

~

What I did in 1945 was mostly a mental achievement.[4]

~

If you lose your desire in anything, you don't do it as well.[5]

~

If I played a bad shot during a round, I didn't worry. I never lost my concentration.[6]

COMPETITION

I had an aggressive attitude when I went out and played.[1]

⟡

In golf you must take an offensive attitude—attack, attack, attack.[2]

⟡

HE'S DETERMINED. EVERY TIME HE PLAYS, WHETHER IT'S A TOURNAMENT OR EXHIBITION, HE TRIES TO SET A RECORD, AND HOW HE HATES TO LOSE! I WAS ON THE TRAIN WITH HIM AFTER HE HAD LOST TO BOB HAMILTON IN THE PGA FINALS LAST SUMMER, AND HE SAID: "I'M GOING TO WIN MY NEXT THREE TOURNAMENTS." AND HE DID.[3]

—*Fred Corcoran*

⟡

I RANK HIM THE NO. 1 COMPETITOR OF ALL. HE HAS THE FIERCEST COMPETITIVE DISPOSITION I'VE EVER KNOWN.[4]

—*Paul Runyan*

THE FACET OF BYRON NELSON'S CHARACTER THAT MOST FASCINATES AND MYSTIFIES ME IS THAT A MAN WITH SUCH REFRESHINGLY SIMPLE TASTES AND A CHRISTIAN ATTITUDE CAN HAVE TURNED HIMSELF AT WILL INTO SUCH A RUTHLESS, RECORD-SETTING GOLF MACHINE, A VERITABLE COLD-EYED TEXAS KILLER OF THE LINKS.[5]

—*Ben Wright*

BYRON IS A SWEET PERSON, BUT HE HAD TO HAVE BEEN A VICIOUS COMPETITOR TO ACHIEVE SUCH A GREAT PLAYING RECORD.[6]

—*Ken Venturi*

I REMEMBERED SOMETHING BYRON HAD TAUGHT ME: NO
MATTER WHAT, NEVER LET YOUR OPPONENT KNOW YOUR
FEELINGS, THAT HIS SHOT OVERWHELMED YOU OR YOUR
OWN SHOT ELATED YOU. SOMETHING ELSE I SAW THAT DAY:
AS A COMPETITOR, BYRON NELSON WAS ABLE TO BE MEAN
AND TOUGH AND INTIMIDATING—AND PLEASANT.[7]

—*Ken Venturi*

I remember how, in the years when we had a lot of
match-play tournaments, I'd get an opponent two or
three holes down, start to feel sorry for him, and
unconsciously slack off in my own play. The first thing
I knew he'd have me by the seat of the pants and I was
beaten. It didn't take me long to get over that attitude,
and it's something you should work to avoid.[8]

Back in the old days, when Ben and Sam and I were tearing golf courses apart, I had only one idea: If I was shooting three strokes under par, I'd keep saying to myself, "You gotta get another birdie. You gotta make it four under."[9]

NELSON CHEWS YOU UP AND SPITS YOU OUT—HOW CAN ANYONE BEAT HIM?[10]

—*Mike Turnesa*

I have big hands but with a lot of feel. The Lord gave me good coordination, a great rhythm, and wonderful balance. I had an absolutely uncanny judgment of distance. And even though folks couldn't always see it, I had a very big desire to achieve. I got pretty steamed up inside.[11]

FROM HIS EARLIEST DAYS AS A TOURNAMENT GOLFER, BYRON NELSON HAD A DISTINCT REPUTATION. HE WAS THE TEXT-BOOK SOUTHERN GENTLEMAN IN A PROFESSION GENEROUSLY STOCKED WITH HARD-BITTEN COMPETITORS AND MORE THAN A FEW PRIMA DONNAS. NOT THAT HE WAS A PUSHOVER IN THE SCRIMMAGE. QUITE THE CONTRARY. HE'D BLOW YOU AWAY IN A HEARTBEAT, YET SMILE POLITELY, IF NOT APOLO-GETICALLY, AS HE HELPED YOU PICK UP THE PIECES.[12]

—*Irwin Smallwood, writer*

HE WAS A TOUGH NUT, TOUGH COMPETITOR, BUT HE DIDN'T HANG AROUND MUCH WITH SOME OF US. HE DIDN'T DRINK, HE DIDN'T CAROUSE, HE DIDN'T STAY OUT LATE AT NIGHT LIKE SOME OF US. HE'D JUST GO HOME AT NIGHT. YOU KNOW, HE JUST DIDN'T HAVE ANY FUN AT ALL.[13]

—*Sam Snead*

Snead's funny, isn't he? But when Sam says I didn't have any fun, he's wrong. Sam, you really think winning eighteen tournaments in one year wasn't any fun?[14]

⌒

The Lord hates a coward.[15]
> —*Nelson to himself during his 1937 Masters victory*

⌒

Winners are different. They're a different breed of cat. I think the reason is, they have an inner drive and are willing to give of themselves whatever it takes to win. It's a discipline that a lot of people are not willing to impose on themselves. It takes a lot of energy, a different way of thinking. It makes a different demand on you to win tournaments than to just go out and win money.[16]

⌒

It's just like I've got the ball on the clubface and am just reaching out with it and laying it by the pin. Now understand, this isn't egotism, a feeling that nobody can beat me. But it's a feeling that they've got to beat my best before I settle up.[17]

⁓

Nelson confessed that he preferred to go into the last round one stroke behind rather than slightly ahead:

The pressure is on the fellow that's out in front. And after all, one stroke is nothing to make up in eighteen holes. It works this way with me—if I'm a little in front, I start playing defensively to hold the lead. And when I start trying to play everything safe I can't do anything. But if I'm a little behind, I start to gamble a little and things start going right.[18]

⁓

Speaking for myself, I don't think a fellow should plan to win 'em all. Certainly he should play as well as he is able every day, and many times he will be astonished to see how well everything falls together.[19]

There's nothing as exciting in golf as playing for your country.[20]

I had a whole collection of goals I wanted to reach, and every good shot I hit supported all of them.[21]

There's nothing as exciting in golf as playing for your country.

A good player loves to compete, loves to win, and hates to lose. You show me a good loser and I'll show you somebody who doesn't win much.[22]

Once you've been a tough competitor—and I think I was—it's the most difficult thing in the world to accept mediocrity. I play now because I enjoy being with my friends.[23]

TEACHING THE GAME

I HAVE NEVER HEARD OF HIM TURNING DOWN ANYONE WHO
WANTED ADVICE.[1]

—*Ross T. Collins, PGA professional*

My philosophy of teaching, even when I taught poor
players, is that you never try to do too many things at
a time.[2]

SO I SHOT 66. WE WENT INSIDE AND HAD SOME SOFT DRINKS.
I WAS WAITING FOR BYRON TO TELL ME HOW GOOD I WAS. I
KEPT WAITING UNTIL FINALLY I COULDN'T STAND IT ANY
LONGER. I SAID, "WHAT DO YOU THINK, MR. NELSON?" HE
SAID, "THAT WAS A GREAT ROUND, KEN, YOU PLAYED WELL.
I'LL MEET YOU OUT HERE TOMORROW MORNING AT NINE
O'CLOCK. THERE ARE ABOUT SEVEN OR EIGHT THINGS WE'VE
GOT TO WORK ON."[3]

—*Ken Venturi*

HE WELCOMES A STEADY STREAM OF GOLFERS SEEKING HIS HELP. HE'S LIKE A GOLF DOCTOR. YOU'LL SEE VENTURI, RAGAN, MAYER, ROMACK—A JILLION OF THEM STOPPING BY TO TALK.[4]

—*Jim Chambers, retired publisher*

The best teachers in my opinion were those who had taught themselves how to play, and who also had the ability to take it slow and easy with amateurs and be very patient.[5]

HE CAME UP TO ME AFTER THAT LAST ROUND AT WINGED FOOT AND SPENT ABOUT FIVE OR TEN MINUTES WITH ME. TOLD ME NOT TO GET DOWN. TOLD ME IF I EVER WANTED ANY HELP HE WOULD WORK WITH ME.[6]

—*Tom Watson*

*Byron counts Tom Watson among many of his
golfing friends he has been honored to mentor over the
years. (Photo courtesy of Salesmanship Club of Dallas)*

I WENT DOWN TO TEXAS IN THE FALL OF 1976, AND WE
WORKED. AND IT JUST SO HAPPENS IT COINCIDES WITH THE
BEGINNING OF MY CAREER, 1977, WHEN I STARTED WINNING
A LOT OF GOLF TOURNAMENTS.[7]

—*Tom Watson*

I have seen a lot of players who were fine golfers and
knew a great deal about the game from a technical
standpoint go to someone, or listen to someone, who
knew less about the game than the questioner did. The
result usually is bad.[8]

When Kenny (Venturi) became such a good player, all
of a sudden I got a reputation of being a good teacher.
Someone asked me about it not too long ago how I got
such a good reputation, and I said, "I pick good
pupils."[9]

I don't do any formal instruction, but a lot of fellows on the tour seem to think I have a knack for picking out little things that might be wrong with their game or swing. I'm always more than happy to help them.[10]

BEN HOGAN

BYRON'S GOT A GOOD GAME, BUT IT'D BE A LOT BETTER IF
HE'D PRACTICE. HE'S TOO LAZY TO PRACTICE.[1]

—*Ben Hogan*

Back then the tour was different than it is now. A lot
of us pros drove from tournament to tournament in a
kind of caravan, and right after Phoenix, which hap-
pened to end on my birthday that year, we all headed
for Texas. Ben and Valerie Hogan and Louise and I
liked to stick together, so we'd follow each other pretty
closely on the road. You kind of had to do that,
because if you had car trouble, it was good to have a
buddy nearby to help you fix a flat or whatever.[2]

Snead tells the story about Ben and me rooming
together and me leaping out of bed in the middle of
the night hearing rats. Ben told me to go back to bed.
It was only him gnashing his teeth.[3]

Ben Hogan has said that the boys today don't enjoy the game as much as we did, which is quite a statement coming from a man as serious about his golf as Ben always has been, and I believe there's something to that.[4]

~

HOGAN HAD A PSYCHOLOGICAL DISADVANTAGE WHEN FACING NELSON. BEN WAS JEALOUS OF HIM. NELSON DIDN'T HAVE A JEALOUS BONE IN HIS BODY.[5]

—*Paul Runyan*

~

I DON'T THINK BEN HOGAN EVER GOT THE BEST OF HIM.[6]

—*Sam Snead*

~

NELSON COULD HIT IRON SHOTS THAT MADE A RULER SEEM
CROOKED. HE RARELY DROVE THE BALL OUT OF PLAY—NELSON
USED TO LISTEN TO HOGAN TALK ABOUT DRAWING OR FADING
A SHOT INTO A GREEN. BYRON WOULD SAY, "WHY DON'T YOU
JUST HIT IT STRAIGHT AT THE HOLE?"[7]

—Ken Venturi

Ben and I were always competitors. Ben had just shot
a 261, and that was a new record, and I started hot at
Seattle and stayed hot for the whole tournament. The
259 was not as many under par as Ben's 261, but I got
a great kick out of it.[8]

WHEN HOGAN DID SOMETHING REMARKABLE, NELSON
INVARIABLY CAME UP WITH A MATCHING PERFORMANCE,
AND VICE VERSA.[9]

—*Herbert Warren Wind, writer*

Ben has never liked being around a lot of people and that's fine. It's his business and I respect that.[10]

~

We've always gotten along fine and we've always liked each other very much. We're simply different personalities, and there's nothing wrong with that.[11]

~

THE (MASTERS) PLAY-OFF OF 1942 IN WHICH
BYRON NELSON DEFEATED BEN HOGAN HAS LONG
REMAINED IN MY MIND AS ONE OF THE MOST
MAGNIFICENT GOLFING CONTESTS I HAVE EVER
WITNESSED.[12]

—*Bobby Jones*

TO MY WAY OF THINKING, YOU FELLOWS (HOGAN
AND NELSON) PUT ON ONE OF THE GREATEST SHOWS
THAT GOLF HAS EVER KNOWN (1942 MASTERS), AND I
WISH I COULD HAVE SOME MORE ADEQUATE MEANS
AT MY DISPOSAL TO EXPRESS OUR APPRECIATION.[13]

—*Clifford Roberts*

THE BYRON NELSON CLASSIC

So many people ask me what it's like having a tournament with my name on it, that I sometimes feel kind of funny about the whole thing. The best way to explain it is just to say that it's one of the best things that has ever happened to me in all my time in golf.[1]

～

Before that call from Felix (McKnight), though, I had done my own homework on the Salesmanship Club and found them to be a dedicated group of men with the most successful children's rehabilitation program that I'd ever heard of. So I agreed to do it, and it's become the best thing that's ever happened to me in golf, better than winning the Masters or the U.S. Open or eleven in a row. Because it helps people.[2]

～

Tom Watson, who has won the Nelson Classic four times, was asked why he plays so consistently well in the event:

"MAYBE," HE SAID, A SMILE CREASING HIS FRECKLED FACE, "LORD BYRON INSPIRES ME."[3]

—*Tom Watson*

~

It really makes me feel humble to realize how blessed I am when I see these kids who have problems, and I had a home life that was perfect.[1]

~

This tournament has meant more to keep my name alive and keep me involved in golf than any one thing.[5]

~

HE MIGHT BE AN EVEN BETTER PERSON THAN HE WAS A GOLFER. THE STRONG FIELD HERE IS A TRIBUTE TO HIM. HOPEFULLY, IT WILL BE THE BYRON NELSON CLASSIC FOREVER.[6]

—*John Cook*

~

There is something that makes me feel lots better than having people recognize me because of my television work, though. It has to do with a group of men called the Salesmanship Club, a couple of golf courses, and children who need a lot of help.[7]

~

Having been a pro and around tournaments all my life, I told them, "The only way you're going to have a successful tournament is for the pros' wives to be happy."[8]

~

No event on the tour has a nursery, and a lot of the pros have little children they need to bring along, so we need to start one—that'll help a lot.[9]

~

A tip of the hat to an appreciative audience. (Photo courtesy of Salesmanship Club of Dallas)

I believe the main reason we've always gotten such good support for the tournament is because people realize that every cent of the profits goes to these children and their families, and no one takes any money out for themselves. I don't get a penny, never have, nor does the club president or the tournament chairman. I've always been fortunate to be connected with people who are substantial, who know how to get things done and who do them honestly and properly. And the Salesmanship Club is the best example I've ever seen of these kinds of qualities.[10]

LIFE AFTER EIGHTY

WE SHOULD ALL AGE SO MARVELOUSLY.[1]

— Bob Verdi, writer

⌒

I am more proud of the way people feel about me and the friends that I have than I am about my golf career.[2]

⌒

When you get to be my age, you're just happy to be able to still play.[3]

⌒

I've been wined and dined. Well, I've been dined. I don't wine.[4]

⌒

I'm a woodworker. I make a lot of things.[5]

HOW MANY EIGHTY-TWO-YEAR-OLD MEN DO YOU KNOW
WHO HAVE THEIR OWN LINE OF FINE CLOTHING? FOR THAT
MATTER, HOW MANY EIGHTY-TWO-YEAR-OLD MEN DO YOU
KNOW WHO ARE ACTIVELY INVOLVED WITH RUNNING A PGA
TOUR EVENT, HAVE WRITTEN AN AUTOBIOGRAPHY, STARTED A
GOLF SCHOOL, HELPED DESIGN GOLF COURSES, RECENTLY
FINISHED A GOLF INSTRUCTION VIDEO, AND TRAVEL FROM
ONE END OF THE COUNTRY TO THE OTHER MAKING APPEAR-
ANCES, GIVING SPEECHES, AND SERVING AS GOLF'S GOOD-
WILL AMBASSADOR? MEET BYRON NELSON OF THE 1990S.[6]

—*Ron Balicki, writer*

NELSON'S HOME REMAINS SIMPLE. "WE DON'T HAVE A DISH-
WASHER," HE SAYS. "I'M THE DISHWASHER."[7]

—*Ivan Maisel, writer*

HE HAS A BAD HIP, BIFOCALS, AND THE EXCEEDINGLY RARE
SUPERSTAR'S OPINION THAT THE WORLD WAS NOT CREATED
FOR HIM, EVEN THOUGH HE DRAMATICALLY CHANGED IT.[8]

—*Ric Weber, writer*

BYRON MENTIONED HE HAD NEVER PLAYED WITH A GLOVE AND WANTED TO KNOW IF I DID. I USED ONE BUT SAID I DIDN'T. THEN HE ASKED ME IF I WANTED CREAM IN MY COFFEE. HE SAID HE LIKED IT BLACK, SO, EVEN THOUGH I ALWAYS TOOK CREAM, I ANSWERED I LIKED MINE BLACK, TOO.[9]

—*Peggy Nelson*

I had a list of sixteen points and said it was important to me to know how she (Peggy) felt. And after I reviewed them all, I asked her if she was still interested in me and she answered yes.[10]

Peggy says it's a good thing she's just fifty years old, because she wouldn't be able to keep up with me. But I blame it (busy schedule) on her. I like to kid her about it. I tell her I wasn't doing very much before, "And all of a sudden I marry you and everybody wants to see you, so here we go."[11]

She (Peggy) tells me, "You're the youngest eighty-two-year-old man I know." And I tell her, "You helped me with that."[12]

⁓

I'M IN LOVE WITH THIS OLD GUY.[13]

—*Peggy Nelson*

⁓

BYRON HAS THE MOST WONDERFUL FRIENDS. ABOUT TEN THOUSAND CLOSE FRIENDS, AT LAST COUNT.[14]

—*Peggy Nelson*

⁓

The great thing is I'm a man who did something fifty years ago, and I'm still here to talk about it. When did you ever hear about something like that in sports?[15]

⁓

HE'LL LATCH ON TO A PIECE OF FURNITURE YOU WOULDN'T
PAY FIFTEEN CENTS FOR, POLISH AND CARESS IT UNTIL IT'S
WORTH THREE HUNDRED DOLLARS. HE'S A PERFECT PERFEC-
TIONIST WITH HIS RANCH.[16]

—*Jim Chambers, retired publisher*

Most of the time I'd rather do woodwork than play
golf anymore, because I can't play golf all that well
these days, and when I do play, it makes me hurt just
about everywhere. But when I work in my shop I have
something to show for my time, and beautiful wood is
really satisfying to work with. I love it.[17]

I am exactly happy. I got what I wanted from golf. I've
had a good, warm, inward feeling all my life.[18]

TO THIS DAY, HE'S A HAPPY FELLOW, VERY MUCH INVOLVED IN HIS RANCHING, HIS CHURCH ACTIVITIES, HIS TOURNAMENT— THE BYRON NELSON CLASSIC—AND ITS CHARITIES. HE ACCOMPLISHED ALL OF HIS GOALS, AND NOT MANY PEOPLE CAN SAY THAT.[19]

—*Sam Snead*

I've never known a man who has been blessed as I have.[20]

I hope people will say I was a good man who did right. I would hope they would remember that I did play good golf for a period of time. The most important thing is to have people see that I've been reliable and have been good for the game of golf as well as a good citizen.[21]

HE IS CONSIDERED TO BE ONE OF THE GREATEST GOLFERS. HE
WILL BE REMEMBERED MUCH MORE SO FOR THE WAY HE
LIVED HIS LIFE AND HOW HE TRIED TO HELP PEOPLE IN ANY
WAY HE COULD.[22]

—*Ben Crenshaw*

I still feel one of these days I'm going to be like Rip
Van Winkle and wake up to find it's been a good, long
dream.[23]

I feel like I'm the luckiest man in golf. Not just
because I have a few records attached to my name or
anything like that. Just because of the way people have
accepted me, wherever I've gone, welcomed me.[24]

Be the best you can be at whatever you do. Be the best
golfer you can be. Be the best businessman you can be.
Be the best husband you can be.[25]

I've had a
wonderful life.[26]

FRIENDS

IN 1953 AND '54, WE PLAYED A LOT OF EXHIBITIONS TOGETHER.
WHEN WE ARRIVED AT THE FIRST TEE, BYRON WOULD ALWAYS
ASK WHAT THE COURSE RECORD WAS AND WHO HELD IT. I
WAS PUZZLED BY THIS THE FIRST TIME HE DID IT AND ASKED
HIM WHY HE WANTED TO KNOW. HE REPLIED, "AS LONG AS
YOU PLAY WITH ME, KEN, REMEMBER ONE THING: YOU NEVER
BREAK THE COURSE RECORD IF IT'S OWNED BY THE HOST PRO,
BECAUSE HE LIVES THERE AND YOU'RE ONLY VISITING." WE
BOTH HAD NUMEROUS CHANCES TO BREAK COURSE RECORDS,
BUT NEVER DID.[1]

—Ken Venturi

ONE YEAR NELSON WROTE TO (DAVIS) LOVE NOT ONLY TO ASK
HIM TO PLAY, BUT ALSO TO INVITE HIM AND FRED COUPLES TO
DINNER AT FAIRWAY RANCH, WHERE NELSON HAS LIVED SINCE
HE GAVE UP THE TOUR IN 1946. LOVE CALLS THE EVENING
"ONE OF THE GREATEST THINGS I'VE DONE IN MY LIFE."[2]

—Ivan Maisel, *writer*

I'M SURE GLAD I DIDN'T HAVE TO PLAY AGAINST YOU WHEN
YOU WERE YOUNG.[3]

—*Gary Player*

Now along comes Tiger. I think the reason Tiger Woods
is so fantastically popular is his name, the way he's come
from behind to win so many golf tournaments.[4]

ONE OTHER THING I WAS TAUGHT BY MY FATHER WAS THAT
GOLF IS A GAME FOR GENTLEMEN. AND I CAN'T THINK OF A
NICER GENTLEMAN IN OUR SPORT THAN BYRON NELSON. I'M
ONLY SORRY WE WERE FROM DIFFERENT GENERATIONS—IT
WOULD HAVE BEEN FUN TO COMPETE AGAINST HIM.[5]

—*Arnold Palmer*

HE TRAVELED WITH LOUISE, BUT WHEN SHE WENT HOME,
HE TRAVELED WITH ME. WE NEVER QUARRELED FROM 1933
TO 1947.[6]

—*Jug McSpaden*

Fortunately, I never was particularly hard to get along with.[7]

⁓

IF I'M AN AUTHORITY ON GOLF, IT'S BECAUSE I WAS TAUGHT BY BYRON NELSON AND PLAYED WITH BEN HOGAN—BYRON IS THE FINEST GENTLEMAN I'VE EVER KNOWN. I JUST LOVE THE MAN.[8]

—*Ken Venturi*

⁓

EVEN WHEN NELSON IS ONLY HALFWAY PUTTING, HE CAN'T BE BEATEN. HE PLAYS GOLF SHOTS LIKE A VIRTUOSO. THERE IS NO PROBLEM HE CAN'T HANDLE—HIGH SHOTS, LOW SHOTS, WITH THE WIND OR ACROSS IT, HOOKS OR FADES, HE HAS ABSOLUTE CONTROL OF THE BALL. HE IS THE FINEST GOLFER I HAVE EVER SEEN.[9]

—*Tommy Armour*

⁓

AT MY BEST I NEVER CAME CLOSE TO THE GOLF NELSON SHOOTS.[10]

—*Bobby Jones*

⁓

Ike (General Dwight Eisenhower) was a good man to play golf with. He liked to chat, was very friendly like, and when he'd hit a good shot, that expressive face he had would just beam all over. But when he hit a bad shot, he'd fuss at himself just like the rest of us.[11]

⌒

Cliff Roberts, who ran the (Masters) tournament then, suggested CBS hire me when they became unhappy with whom they had. Roberts told them, "I don't know what Byron'll say, but he won't go off half-cocked."[12]

⌒

Roone Arledge, our producer, right away started telling me I needed to change the way I spoke and quite a few of my expressions. But Chris (Schenkel) told me, "Don't pay any attention, Pro. People who know you know the way you speak, and you speak very plainly. It wouldn't be you if you tried to speak like an Easterner."[13]

⌒

HE'S ALWAYS MAKING APPEARANCES AT TOURNAMENTS. AND
HE'S BECOME A REALLY GOOD FRIEND TO A LOT OF PLAYERS.[14]

—*Phil Mickelson*

BYRON NELSON'S WRITING, HIS IDEAS ABOUT THE GOLF
SWING AND THE WAY HE'D COME UP THROUGH THE GAME
FROM THE CADDIE YARD TO STARDOM AND TREATED THE
GAME WITH SUCH PERSONAL GRACE, ALSO HAD A TREMEN-
DOUS INFLUENCE ON ME.[15]

—*Arnold Palmer*

I'M A VERY SMALL CHAPTER IN JOHN BYRON NELSON'S LIFE,
BUT BYRON IS A VERY LARGE CHAPTER IN THE LIFE OF TOM
WATSON.[16]

—*Tom Watson*

GOLF HAS NEVER HAD A NICER CHAMPION.[17]

—*Jack Nicklaus*

*At home, at peace. (Photo from personal collection of
Byron Nelson)*

NOTES

The Game

1. Chieger, Bob, and Pat Sullivan, *Inside Golf: Quotations on the Royal and Ancient Game.* New York: Antheneum, 1986.
2. Ibid.
3. Ibid.
4. *Golf Digest,* May 1959.
5. 1990 Byron Nelson Classic program.
6. Wade, Don, *Talking on Tour: The Best Anecdotes from Golf's Master Storyteller.* New York: Contemporary Books, 2001.
7. 1998 GTE Byron Nelson Classic program.
8. Nelson, Byron, *Byron Nelson: The Little Black Book.* Arlington, TX: Summit Publishing Group, 1995.
9. Ibid.
10. Anderson, Dave, *The Met Golfer,* Summer 1986.
11. *Corporate Golfer,* May 1995.
12. Nelson, Byron, *Shape Your Swing the Modern Way.* Norwalk, CT: A Golf Digest Book, 1976.
13. Ibid.
14. Ibid.
15. Ibid.
16. Ibid.
17. Ibid.
18. Ibid.
19. Ibid.
20. Ibid.
21. Ibid.
22. Ibid.
23. Ibid.
24. Ibid.
25. Ibid.
26. Ibid.
27. *Golf Journal,* May/June 1986.

28. Nelson, Byron, *Shape Your Swing the Modern Way*. Norwalk, CT: A Golf Digest Book, 1976.
29. *Collier's* August 1945 article reprinted in *The Classics of Golf*, edited by Herbert Warren Wind, published by Ailsa in 1991.
30. June 1948 *Golfing* article reprinted in *The Classics of Golf*, edited by Herbert Warren Wind, published by Ailsa in 1991.
31. Ibid.
32. Ibid.
33. Ibid.
34. *Philadelphia Bulletin*, June 13, 1939.
35. Ibid.
36. *Golf Digest*, March 1970.
37. *Philadelphia Bulletin*, March 23, 1940.
38. *Philadelphia Bulletin*, June 18, 1945.
39. *Philadelphia Bulletin*, January 26, 1969.
40. Ibid.
41. *Philadelphia Bulletin*, April 2, 1963.
42. Nelson, Byron, *Byron Nelson: The Little Black Book*. Arlington, TX: Summit Publishing Group, 1995.
43. *Dallas Times Herald*, May 4, 1989.
44. Nelson, Byron, *How I Played the Game*. Dallas: Taylor Publishing Company, 1993.
45. *Golf Magazine*, February 1960.
46. Ibid.
47. Ibid.
48. *Golf Magazine*, June 1960.
49. Ibid.
50. Nelson, Byron, *Byron Nelson: The Little Black Book*. Arlington, TX: Summit Publishing Group, 1995.
51. *Golf Magazine*, June 1960.
52. *Byron Nelson, The Story of Golf's Finest Gentleman and the Greatest Winning Streak in History*. New York: The American Golfer/Broadway Books, 1997.
53. *Golfing*, June 1954.
54. Ibid.
55. Ibid.
56. Ibid.

Notes

57. Ibid.
58. Ibid.
59. *Golf Magazine*, May 1959.

The Streak
1. *Golf Digest*, May 1995.
2. Ibid.
3. Nelson, Byron, *The Story of Golf's Finest Gentleman and the Greatest Winning Streak in History*. New York: The American Golfer/Broadway Books, 1997.
4. Ibid.
5. Ibid.
6. *Braniff International Travel Magazine*, Volume 10, Number 8, 1981.
7. Snead, Sam, with Fran Pirozzolo, *The Game I Love*. New York: Ballantine Books, 1997.
8. Anderson, Dave, *The Met Golfer*, Summer 1986.
9. Nelson, Byron, *Byron Nelson: The Little Black Book*. Arlington, TX: Summit Publishing Group, 1995.
10. Ibid.
11. Ibid.
12. *Golfweek*, January 14, 1995.
13. Ibid.
14. *Dallas Morning News*, May 13, 1994.
15. *Golf World*, April 28, 1995.
16. Hauser, Thomas, with Arnold Palmer, *Arnold Palmer: A Personal Journey*. San Francisco: Collins Publishers, 1994.
17. Nelson, Byron, *The Byron Nelson Story*. Cincinnati, OH: Old Golf Shop, Inc., 1980.
18. *Wichita Falls Times-Record News*, May 7, 1993.
19. Ibid.
20. *The Oregonian*, date unknown.
21. *Sports Illustrated*, May 7, 1979.
22. *Charlotte Observer*, March 19, 1995.
23. *Dallas Morning News*, August 6, 1990.
24. *On Tour*, May 1995.
25. *Los Angeles Times*, March 11, 1995.

26. Hauser, Melanie, ed., *Under the Lone Star Flagstick: A Collection of Writings on Texas Golf and Golfers*. New York: Simon & Schuster, 1997.
27. *USA Today*, May 15, 1997.
28. *Sports Illustrated*, July 10, 1995.
29. Nelson, Byron, *How I Played the Game*. Dallas: Taylor Publishing Company, 1993.
30. Wind, Herbert Warren, *The Story of American Golf: Its Champions and Its Championships*. New York, NY: Alfred A. Knopf, Inc., 1975.
31. *Dallas Morning News*, July 3, 1988.
32. *Dallas Morning News*, March 7, 1995.

Love of Golf

1. Excerpts from a 1945 newspaper interview republished in Byron Nelson Testimonial Dinner program, April 23, 1968.
2. *Corporate Golfer*, May 1995.
3. Nelson, Byron, *Byron Nelson: The Little Black Book*. Arlington, TX: Summit Publishing Group, 1995.
4. Nelson, Byron, *Shape Your Swing the Modern Way*, a Golf Digest Book, 1976.
5. Pat Seelig column, publication unknown, 1989.
6. *Dallas Times Herald*, May 4, 1989.
7. Nelson, Byron, *Shape Your Swing the Modern Way*, a Golf Digest Book, 1976.
8. *On Tour*, March 1995.
9. *Dallas Morning News*, August 6, 1990.
10. *USA Today*. May 15, 1997.
11. Seelig, Pat, *Historic Golf Courses of America*. Dallas: Taylor Publishing Company, 1994.
12. Nelson, Byron, *How I Played the Game*. Dallas: Taylor Publishing Company, 1993.
13. Ibid.
14. *Golf Digest*, June 1965.
15. *Dallas Morning News*, May 5, 1979.

Faith

1. *Links*, March/April 1995.
2. *ACU Today*, Summer 1984.
3. *Links*, March/April 1995.

Notes

4. Sheard, Jim, and Wally Armstrong, *Finishing the Course: Strategies for the Back Nine of Your Life*. Nashville, TN: J Countryman, a Thomas Nelson Co., 2000.
5. *Dallas Morning News*, February 16, 1992.
6. *ACU Today*, Spring 1993.
7. Ibid.
8. Hauser, Melanie, ed., *Under the Lone Star Flagstick: A Collection of Writings on Texas Golf and Golfers*. New York: Simon & Schuster, 1997.
9. Nelson, Byron, *How I Played the Game*. Dallas: Taylor Publishing Company, 1993.
10. *Corporate Golfer*, May 1995.

Caddies
1. Excerpt from a 1945 newspaper interview republished in Byron Nelson Testimonial Dinner program, April 23, 1968.
2. 1988 Byron Nelson Classic program.
3. Pat Seelig column, publication unknown, 1989.
4. Alliss, Peter, *Supreme Champions of Golf*. New York: Charles Scribner's Sons, 1986.
5. Nelson, Byron, *Shape Your Swing the Modern Way*, a Golf Digest Book, 1976.

Golf in the Early Years
1. Bisher, Furman, *The Masters*. Birmingham, AL: Oxmoor House, 1976.
2. *Golfing*, June 1948.
3. Nelson, Byron, *How I Played the Game*. Dallas: Taylor Publishing Company, 1993.
4. Ibid.
5. Barkow, Al, *Gettin' to the Dance Floor: An Oral History of American Golf*. Short Hills, NJ: Buford Books, 1986.
6. The 1990 U.S. Senior Open Championship program.
7. *Southern Links*, July/August 1990.
8. Quoted from the *Philadelphia Evening Bulletin*. Reprinted in *The Byron Nelson Story*. Cincinnati, OH: Old Golf Shop, Inc., 1980.
9. Nelson, Byron, *How I Played the Game*. Dallas: Taylor Publishing Company, 1993.
10. *Golf Journal*, March/April 1994.
11. Nelson, Byron, *Byron Nelson: The Little Black Book*. Arlington, TX: Summit Publishing Group, 1995.
12. *San Antonio Express News*, October 8, 1987.
13. Bisher, Furman, *The Masters*.

14. Ibid.
15. Nelson, Byron, *How I Played the Game*. Dallas: Taylor Publishing Company, 1993.

The Tour
1. *ACU Today*, Spring 1993.
2. Nelson, Byron, *The Byron Nelson Story*. Cincinnati, OH: Old Golf Shop, Inc., 1980.
3. Nelson, Byron, *How I Played the Game*. Dallas: Taylor Publishing Company, 1993.
4. Ibid.
5. *ACU Today*, Spring 1993.
6. Anderson, Dave, *The Met Golfer*, Summer 1986.
7. *Chicago Tribune*, April 9, 1989.
8. *Dallas Morning News*, Tuesday, March 7, 1995.
9. Rosaforte, Tim, *Raising The Bar*. New York: Thomas Dunne Books, 2000.
10. *Golf World*, March 19, 1982.

His Career in Golf
1. Nelson, Byron, *How I Played the Game*. Dallas: Taylor Publishing Company, 1993.
2. *Golf World*, January 20, 1995.
3. *Golf Digest*, May 1975.
4. *Golf Magazine*, January 1975.
5. *Southern Links*, July/August 1990.
6. *Golf Digest*, August 1962.
7. *Southern Links*, July/August 1990.
8. Wade, Don, *And Then Jack Said to Arnie: A Collection of the Greatest True Golf Stories of All Time*. Chicago: Contemporary Books, Inc., 1991.

Early Retirement
1. *Dallas Morning News*, February 16, 1992.
2. *Daily Oklahoman*, September 5, 1946.
3. *Golf Digest*, June 1965.
4. *Daily Oklahoman*, September 5, 1946.
5. Ibid.
6. *Golf Digest*, June 1965.

Notes

7. *Golf World*, January 1995.
8. Snead, Sam, with Fran Pirozzolo, *The Game I Love*. New York: Ballantine Books, 1997.
9. *Southern Links*, July/August 1990.
10. *Golf Course Management*, December 1993.
11. *Sports Illustrated*, May 7, 1979.
12. *Golf World*, January 1995.
13. Ibid.

Straight Down the Middle

1. *Golf Digest*, June 1965.
2. *Chicago Daily Tribune*, April 14, 1945.
3. Ibid.
4. Nelson, Byron, *The Story of Golf's Finest Gentleman and the Greatest Winning Streak in History*. New York: The American Golfer/Broadway Books, 1997.
5. Nicklaus, Jack, with Ken Bowden, *My Story*. New York: Simon & Schuster, 1997.
6. *Columbus Citizen Journal*, May 22, 1980, reprinted in *The Byron Nelson Story*. Cincinnati, OH: Old Golf Shop, Inc., 1980.
7. Nelson, Byron, *Byron Nelson: The Little Black Book*. Arlington, TX: Summit Publishing Group, 1995.
8. Nelson, Byron, *Shape Your Swing the Modern Way*. Norwalk, CT: A Golf Digest Book, 1976.
9. Wind, Herbert Warren, *The Story of American Golf: Its Champions and Its Championships*. New York: Alfred A. Knopf, 1975.
10. *Golf Magazine*, June 1972.
11. *Byron Nelson: The Story of Golf's Finest Gentleman and the Greatest Winning Streak in History*.
12. *Golf Digest*, July 2000.
13. Wade, Don, *Talking on Tour: The Best Anecdotes from Golf's Master Storyteller*. Chicago: Contemporary Books, 2001.

The Mental Game

1. Nelson, Byron, *Shape Your Swing the Modern Way*. Norwalk, CT: A Golf Digest Book, 1976.
2. Ibid.

3. Ibid.
4. *New York Times*, May 11, 1993.
5. *Wichita Falls Times-Record News*, May 7, 1993.
6. *Dallas Morning News*, August 6, 1990.

Competition

1. *Corporate Golfer*, May 1995.
2. *Philadelphia Bulletin*, July 2, 1961.
3. *Chicago Daily Tribune*, April 14, 1945.
4. Byron Nelson, *The Story of Golf's Finest Gentleman and the Greatest Winning Streak in History*. New York: The American Golfer/Broadway Books, 1997.
5. *Links*, March 1994.
6. *Golf Digest*, July 2000.
7. Nelson, Byron, *Byron Nelson: The Little Black Book*. Arlington, TX: Summit Publishing Group, 1995.
8. Nelson, Byron, *Shape Your Swing the Modern Way*. Norwalk, CT: A Golf Digest Book, 1976.
9. *Philadelphia Bulletin*, July 2, 1961.
10. Aultman, Dick, and Ken Bowden, *The Methods of Golf's Masters*. Toronto: Longman Canada Limited, 1975.
11. *New York Times*, May 11, 1993.
12. *Greensboro News & Record*, April 16, 1995.
13. *Golf World*, February 3, 1995.
14. Ibid.
15. McCord, Robert, *The Quotable Golfer*. New York: Lyons Press, 2000.
16. Barkow, Al, *Gettin' to the Dance Floor: An Oral History of American Golf*. Short Hills, NJ: Buford Books, 1986.
17. *Philadelphia Bulletin*, September 3, 1940.
18. *Philadelphia Bulletin*, December 15, 1941.
19. *Golf Digest*, May 1959.
20. Nelson, Byron, *How I Played the Game*. Dallas: Taylor Publishing Company, 1993.
21. Ibid.
22. Nelson, Byron, *Shape Your Swing the Modern Way*. Norwalk, CT: A Golf Digest Book, 1976.
23. *Golf Digest*, June 1965.

Notes

Teaching the Game
1. *Professional Golfer,* May 1959.
2. 1990 Byron Nelson Classic program.
3. 1995 GTE Byron Nelson Classic program.
4. *Golf Digest,* June 1965.
5. Nelson, Byron, *How I Played the Game.* Dallas: Taylor Publishing Company, 1993.
6. *Golfweek,* January 14, 1995.
7. Ibid.
8. *Golfing,* June 1954.
9. 1990 Byron Nelson Classic program.
10. *Golf Digest,* August 1962.

Ben Hogan
1. Nelson, Byron, *How I Played the Game.* Dallas: Taylor Publishing Company, 1993.
2. Ibid.
3. *Houston Post,* February 11, 1990.
4. *Byron Nelson, The Story of Golf's Finest Gentleman and the Greatest Winning Streak in History.* New York: The American Golfer/Broadway Books, 1997.
5. Brown, Cal, *Masters Memories.* Chelsea, MI: Sleeping Bear Press, 1998.
6. Snead, Sam, with Fran Pirozzolo, *The Game I Love.* New York: Ballantine Books, 1997.
7. *Charlotte Observer,* March 19, 1995.
8. 25th Byron Nelson Classic program.
9. Wind, Herbert Warren, *The Story of American Golf: Its Champions and Its Championships.* New York: Alfred A. Knopf, 1975.
10. Nelson, Byron, *How I Played the Game.* Dallas: Taylor Publishing Company, 1993.
11. Ibid.
12. *Golf Digest,* April 1960.
13. Owen, David, *The Making of The Masters.* New York: Simon & Schuster, 1999.

The Byron Nelson Classic
1. *Dallas Times Herald,* May 4, 1989.
2. Nelson, Byron, *How I Played the Game.* Dallas: Taylor Publishing Co., 1993.

3. *Braniff International Travel Magazine*, Volume 10, Number 8, 1981.
4. 1991 Byron Nelson Classic program.
5. *Corporate Golfer*, May 1995.
6. *USA Today*, May 15, 1997.
7. Nelson, Byron, *How I Played the Game*. Dallas: Taylor Publishing Co., 1993.
8. Ibid.
9. Ibid.
10. Ibid.

Life After Eighty
  1. *Chicago Tribune*, April 9, 1989.
  2. 1995 GTE Byron Nelson Classic program.
  3. *Chicago Tribune*, April 9, 1989.
  4. *Dallas Morning News*, February 10, 1999.
  5. *Corporate Golfer*, May 1995.
  6. *Golfweek*, January 14, 1995.
  7. *Sports Illustrated*, May 22, 2000.
  8. Fort Myers Press, February 2, 1998.
  9. *Los Angeles Times*, April 13, 1990.
 10. Ibid.
 11. *Golfweek*, January 14, 1995.
 12. *Golf World*, January 20 1995.
 13. *Los Angeles Times*, April 13, 1990.
 14. *San Antonio Express News*, October 8, 1987.
 15. *Charlotte Observer*, March 19, 1995.
 16. *Golf Digest*, June 1965.
 17. Nelson, Byron, *How I Played the Game*. Dallas: Taylor Publishing Company, 1993.
 18. *New York Times*, May 11, 1993.
 19. Snead, Sam, with Fran Pirozzolo, *The Game I Love*. New York: Ballantine Books, 1997.
 20. *Golf Journal*, May/June 1989.
 21. 1990 U.S. Senior Open Championship program.
 22. 25th Byron Nelson Classic program.
 23. *Charlotte Observer*, March 19, 1995.

Notes

24. Hauser, Melanie, ed., *Under the Lone Star Flagstick: A Collection of Writings on Texas Golf and Golfers*. New York: Simon & Schuster, 1997.
25. *Golf Journal*, May/June 1986.
26. *Dallas Morning News*, February 16, 1992.

Friends

1. *Golf Digest*, July 2000.
2. *Sports Illustrated*, May 22, 2000.
3. Goodner, Ross, *Golf's Greatest: The Legendary World Golf Hall of Famers*. Norwalk, CT: A Golf Digest Book, 1978.
4. 1998 GTE Byron Nelson Classic program.
5. Nelson, Byron, *Byron Nelson: The Little Black Book*. Arlington, TX: Summit Publishing Group, 1995.
6. Ibid.
7. *Southern Links*, July/August 1990.
8. Nelson, Byron, *Byron Nelson: The Little Black Book*. Arlington, TX: Summit Publishing Group, 1995.
9. Aultman, Dick, and Ken Bowden, *The Methods of Golf's Masters*. Toronto: Longman Canada Limited, Toronto, 1975.
10. Ibid.
11. Nelson, Byron, *How I Played the Game*. Dallas: Taylor Publishing Company, 1993.
12. *Golf Magazine*, July 1988.
13. Nelson, Byron, *How I Played the Game*. Dallas: Taylor Publishing Company, 1993.
14. *USA Today*, May 15, 1997.
15. Palmer, Arnold, with James Dodson, *A Golfer's Life*. New York: Ballantine Books, 1999.
16. *Columbus Citizen Journal*, May 22, 1980, article reprinted in *The Byron Nelson Story*. Cincinnati, OH: Old Golf Shop, Inc., 1980.
17. Nicklaus, Jack, with Ken Bowden, *My Story*. New York: Simon & Schuster, 1997.

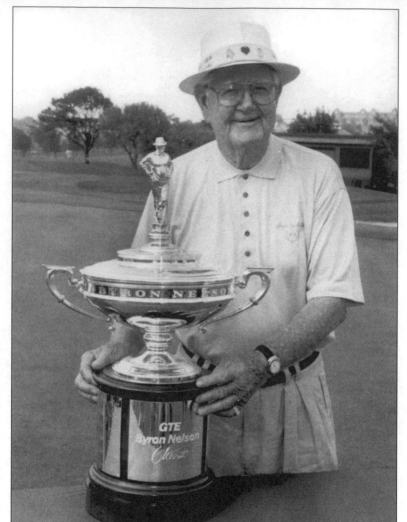